THE INFAMOUS
HISTORY
OF SLAVERY

THE INFAMOUS HISTORY OF SLAVERY

MUSTAFA ABDUS-SALAM

To order additional copies of this book, contact:
Xlibris LLC
1-888-795-4274
www.Xlibris.com
Orders@Xlibris.com
84717

CONTENTS

Dedicated to all the American Indian Nations, Africans, African-Americans, and to the rebirth of the Human Spirit for all of Us . . . We are One Color Humanity!

AUTHOR'S NOTE

In the history of the United States of America there's a contradiction between its reality of democracy, racism and bigotry. Throughout America Democracy, racism and slavery functioned side by side. Whites struggled to build a society based around equality and justice for whites and oppression for blacks. The founding fathers developed a Constitution that embodied equality and justice for whites but maintained oppression and slavery for blacks. That contradiction always bothered me.

Racism throughout America's history was evil and wicked for Blacks. There was always a double standard since the Europeans came to this country. Blacks were constantly being oppressed even when they were fighting to defend this nation as soldiers. George Washington was a great leader but he was also a racist. Justice wasn't for Blacks even when they fought in wars to help maintain freedom and democracy.

It's an Infamous deed to enslave people because they're darker then you. It's an infamous crime when you have a history of continual oppression of any people just because they have some differences then you have. Today people are charged with crimes against humanity for atrocities far less then America's treatment of black people for over five hundred years.

Evaluate as a human being the historical atrocities against black people throughout America's history and let me know if you don't feel the enslavement of blacks isn't infamous. I believe that kidnapping, enslaving, raping and murdering a people any time you feel like it is a terrible historical crime against humanity. A month for 'Black History is not enough" what about inclusion in all books on American History. What about wiping out exclusion and include the historical truth about the participation of Blacks in every battle that occurred from when the settlers first arrive till the present. What about telling the truth about Black Inventors of America, Black's contribution to science, medicine, art, theater, dance, film, ship building, architecture, military development, agriculture, education; why have all the White contribution in American history of everything and then a small section for "Blacks in History".

INTRODUCTION

Infamous means having a very bad reputation, notorious, in disgrace or dishonor. Most whites and even many blacks don't like to discuss slavery. Well open your mind because the bottom line is Blacks are human beings. Racism still exist and its time for all Americans to take a stand against it. Forget about you and think how you'd feel if today some people busted into your home kidnapped you, tied you up, put you in a truck and then a plane. Once at the final place you were subjugated to slavery for the rest of your life. Well now you know how Africans felt! The history is ugly and its America's and we should never forget it, or just think of it as Black history it's American History and its ugly!

Blacks were truly treated terrible by most Whites, so open your mind and let's take a look. Let's walk where Africans traveled and just look and listen. Africans didn't want to be slaves. They didn't want to labor for nothing, be raped, tortured, hung, and murdered. You know today if that crime was played out, the participants in that crime would be international criminals and tried in International Court for Crimes against Humanity! What about what our founding fathers did wasn't it a Crime against Humanity and shouldn't it be remembered as such in the history books. Walk into the pages of history, into the darkness of slavery that so many wish to forget but wait it still plagues us today! There are many Whites who hate people of color for no reason other then their complexion and reverse it, many people of color hate Caucasians for the history and stuff many blacks go through. Underneath our skin we're all basically the same, so when you subjugate one group of people you're committing an inhumane act and it should be offensive to all human beings. Remember if they come for one group today, they can come for another tomorrow, when will we stop racism!

CHAPTER ONE

The Question of Nationality

The White Man is the Caucasian concept of "power" in the world today. Europeans hold the seat of power in the world, in the White House, Congress and Senate. They hold the seat of power the United Nations, in the European business market, and play a big part even in the Asian Business market, Arabian and African Business market. The White man is really a concept not a race; he is the man, the power broker and the one who sit on the throne of world power. That's how most Black sees it, and that's what they mean when they say the 'White man". What do Caucasians mean when they see "those Blacks". They don't see something good, in other words, they see monsters, evil, thieves, murderers and most likely a criminal element. Blacks shouldn't feel nervous to walk down streets but many in the "Ghetto (what the hell does that mean, well to most whites, it means the dirty and criminal black neighborhood) do. Whites started calling Blacks niggers, now Blacks use it as a badge of honor between each other. Things are really getting crazy because in the ghetto (the Black neighborhoods) children and adults are still getting shot daily why? A monster has been created by subjugation, confinement, poor employment and education, racism, exploitation; developing a monster who has no problem to sell her body, sell drugs, utilize drugs, fight and kill each other; the slave has become the exploited and the exploited exploits each other because its safer and easier then to go into the Caucasian community or should I say, evolve get educated, buy a house and live in a clean, comfortable neighborhood even destroy the concept of ghetto and make the neighborhood descend, clean, with minimal crime and businesses owned by different nationalities including

Blacks. The world we live in is the one we create. Black people are no different then whites, Blacks and Whites even fall in love and that to is normal, once the racist and the slave mentally which still lingers in the minds of people of color is eliminated, then we become Americans all of us, not Black or White. In Ancient time, in Rome, Greece, Egypt people were all to relate sexually and politically regardless of your complexion. Power was important; political, social, economic and physical made you important or not. There were Black and White citizens in ancient Rome and Greece. The Egyptians, Romans and Greeks all inter-married; even though in many of those societies being a bastard child excluded you from reaching the throne although many did. The racism that exists today wasn't popular; many Blacks ruled or played a part in ruling many ancient societies. Hannibal the Great was a Black man who dominate Rome and father many children from Roman women.

In a book called 'The Greeks', by Anne Pearson states, "Ancient Greece was never one united country. Although. The Greeks spoke the same language and called themselves Greeks; they belonged to a number of little city-states, each with its own main town, government, army and coinage. The cities competed with one another for land, and trade. Because the land of Greece was so barren, many Greeks immigrated to new colonies, in Asia Minor and all over the Mediterranean." Europeans developed In Europe and Asia, living, working fighting and building city-states among each other, cities like Rome developed and ruled over many other cities, groups/ tribes like Britain's became independent and powerful and their Kingdom conquered and ruled the Irish people, who fought the British for independence throughout history, even today they still haven't completely reached peace. Rome became a city-state and eventually a powerful nation-state with Black, white, Persian and Asian slaves that they captured or caught in war. Slavery existed throughout the Ancient world even among the aboriginal peoples of what became the America's. Slaves in Rome fought as gladiators; Greece also had slaves fighting as gladiators and in the Aztec kingdom most of the slaves were sacrificed to the Gods and worked in the fields.

Slavery existed amongst most ancient people as an institution. The Spanish, British, Chinese, Jews, Arabs, Asians, Aztec's and other Amerindians had slaves. Slavery seems to have been an integral part of the development of most nations and people's of the world. When the Spanish met the Aztec's they too had slaves, most of which they used to sacrifice to their gods. The Spanish were able to conquer them easily and took over their nation enslaving them, using their women for sex because the Conquistadors didn't come with women so they took the Indian women as their mates which created a population of Spanish people everywhere they went. This is the system that created the people we call Mexicans, Peruvian, Ecuadorians, Columbians, and many other Spanish people.

The world we know developed out of struggles between the powerful and the want to be powerful, religious in fighting, such as Muslims and Christians. Europe, Asia and Africa were basically a polytheistic group. Most believed in a group of gods who they worship and gave sacrifices to in terms of food, people, money and other things. The Asiatic religions of Buddhism, Hinduism, Zen Buddhism are older then Christianity. Judaism is one of the oldest monotheistic religions, and then there is Christianity followed by Islam. The Popes and Patriarchs Christianity developed first in Ethiopia, then into Egypt, Rome then Greece, traveling into Eastern Europe. Islam developed in Arabia with the religious mission of Muhammad becoming a Prophet and Messenger of God. Islam then began to travel throughout Arabia and was met harshly by the polytheistic groups who planned Mohammad's demise and when they couldn't murder him, they offered him to become a king which he refused and then offered him wealth. Islam grew throughout Arabia into Africa and Asia, into Eastern Europe and even into Indonesia and China. Christianity flowered in Rome when King Constantine accepts it and the structure of Bishops and Pope were instituted drawing from the system instituted in Ethiopia, Egypt and the Greeks. Conflicts ensued in the Holy City of Bethlehem between Jews, Christians and Muslims. There were in fighting especially between the Christians and Muslims in the Holy Lands for control of the Holy Lands. Islam got control of the Holy lands, in around the 10th Century until the 15th Century, internal wars between the Christians under the Roman Pope and the Islamic group governing Bethlehem started. Pope Urban II, head of the Roman Catholic Church throughout Europe, send Crusaders to stop the Saracens a group of Turkish Muslims from mistreating Christian Pilgrims who wanted to visit their Holy Places there. "There were about four crusades that followed, in 1191 King Richard the Lion Heart led the third Crusade against Saladin and won the last battle they fought but he decided to allow Saladin to continue control of the Holy City after agreeing to allow more freedom for the Christians'. By 1291 the Saracens were once again in control of all of the territory of the Holy Land, and the last crusades had returned to Europe, learning many new lessons from their enemy. The Crusaders learned and copied much of the culture of the Muslims such as the use of carpets, cushions and tapestries, that helped brighten their gloomy castles. They also learned from Eastern discoveries in science and mathematics. For instances the numbers we use today were first developed in the East". Is explained by Joanne Jessop in the Book, "Beginning History, 'Crusades". The development of Religion brought a major amount of organization and unity among different groups who practiced the same religion, although many Arab, Asian and African Muslims enslaved each other and sold them first in the Trans-Saharan Slave trade but later sold basically African and dark Arab slaves in the Tri-Atlantic slave trade that went to Europe and down the Atlantic to the Caribbean and on to the America's by the 1600's in Spanish ships bringing along Africans received on the coast of Africa and began developing the trans-Atlantic slave trade. By 1619, the Dutch traders also began to arrive on the coast with African slaves. Many books will state that Indians first saw Africans when they arrived on the coast as slaves. Many other historical books suggest that Africans arrived in North America from the Ancient African states of Mali and Songhai on ships through the Caribbean current into the Aztec area because there were sculptures of Ole Mecs and homes built like those in Africa were being built when the Spanish arrived. In a Book, "The Black Frontiersmen" by J. Norman Heard states that slaves in the United States were slaves of the Explorers. One of the earliest of these was Estevanico, a Moor who sailed from Cuba with the Narvaez expedition in 1528, was cast away on the Texas coast, and made his way across deserts and mountains to the Pacific coast of Mexico. Later Estevanico discovered Mexico in search of the fabled Seven Cities Cibola." In many events early settlers, even the Blacks that arrived with them met the arrows of the Indians in there early deaths, nevertheless, with their rifles and guns, as well as their horses they were able to push the Indians back and make head ways into their lands. The reason the Moors were used is because the Europeans knew they were intelligent and had skills in agriculture, building, architecture, medicine, and science, etc. Even in book, "The Black Frontiersmen by J. Norman Heard", he suggest, "that some historians believe that a Negro sailed to the New World with Columbus on his first voyage" . . . . He writes this statement as if he doesn't believe it. Well if one reads load of new books by scholars, you'll find that yes an African did arrive with Columbus who was a navigator from the Nina's family who inter-married with a Spanish woman and assimilated into the Islamic community and when necessary into the Spanish society. This family gave a lot of money to the poor Kingdom of Ferdinand and Isabella, as well as helped redevelop its seaport, and shipping industry. They named one of the ships the Nina because of the families' contributions! The Spanish did everything they could to wipe out the Moors historical contributions to Spain. They destroyed buildings, turned Mosque into Churches, wipe out Islamic cemeteries, schools, universities, tapestry, mosaic art throughout Spain, forced families change their names to Spanish ones, although many Spanish names have Arabic names included in them and they've forgotten they are really Arabic names. Spain is right across the Strait of Gibraltar from Morocco and within Tangiers and Spain you can see the cultural influences from each country from the people, dress, languages and the food. Which I loved while I was there looking over to Spain.

Europeans in the 15th century created specific nationalities like Caucasian, Arab, Asian, African, East Indian and Amerindian and Caribou (for Caribbean Indian). These specific racial identities also was to show that Europeans were suppose to be the most developed, while the Arab, Asian and East Indian were the second (including the Yellow man) while the Black and Red Man is the least developed. This was the cleansing process of eliminating all historical contributions of people of color in the psyche, history and culture of Europeans, although they couldn't totally do it. The contributions were everywhere in statutes in Rome (many Roman leaders were Black), Egypt, Spain, Russia (Alexander Pushkin the writer of the 'Three Musketeers was Black), Greece, Persia, Constantinople, Carthrage, Ethiopia, Lebanon, Bethlehem, Asia, India, China all had dark, Vietnam, Korea (all have dark folks) . . .

Once chattel slavery began in the 15th century Whites developed new philosophies which tried to show that Blacks were inferior to Whites: physically, mentally and culturally. To prove this they wiped out most of the Black characters in the Bible and in most history books. They wished to transform Black historical, cultural, religious and artistic figures into white ones throughout history. This was going on in white European Nations as well as colonized Africa and Asia ones. The Buddha began to look darker. African and Asian people became slaves and servants.

Black people were no longer accepted as Human beings in the same category as Whites. Whites even created a place called Negroland where the Negroes came from. They created books, scientific research and papers that proved Black people were scientifically inferior. All of this justified our enslavement and provided them with scientific for enslaving us, so they can help us to become more human. This change in status allowed the Caucasians to feel justified and morally okay for enslaving, beating, caging, murdering and forcing African and many Asian people to comply coercively to satisfy their needs. Once the Christian Whites developed this historical untrue African image they went upon the business of releasing hell upon African and Asian peoples.

CHAPTER TWO

The Onslaught for Power

In the 15th Century Europe were motivated in two directions one towards the new world, and the other toward Africa and Asia for colonialization. Which they thought would be as easy the Spanish colonialization of the Aztecs. Though when they meet the Indians of North America, they were fierce and didn't surrender, run or give up their lands. They fought with organized warriors and in the beginnings caused much harm to the Dutch who arrived in 1619 in a Dutch man of war ship with a large group of African slaves for the English colonies. Slavery had begun to become instituted in the late1500's in the Caribbean and in the America's in the 1600's with British and Dutch.

At the same time that the man of war ships were landing in on the coast of America, other's were rounding the coast of Africa, trading with slave traders for their slaves to bring to the Caribbean, and other British traders, soldiers and missionaries were entering villages, cities and states of Africans to negotiate for land, resources and slaves when possible. For many of the tribes and city-states would sell their captives or even some of their poor in order to obtain needed resources, like weapons, foodstuff, cloth or skins, and tools, etc. More of these people were developing, using rifles, many of the bigger groups like Songhai, Timbuktu, Ghana, the Hausa, etc were using horses, rifles, farming tools, weaving cloth, even building large houses for the Kings and Queens. In many of the Islamic states, they were reading and writing Arabic, many were Islamic scholars, Imams (religious leaders), callers to prayer, and Qur'anic recitter's who would recite the Qur'an after or before prayers. The children, even the women and daughter's in Islamic African societies were taught to read the Qur'an. Many of the women would lead prayer when the men were away at war, hunting, visiting others or just busy. The women would pray among themselves and a woman like Imam would lead prayer. These were very developed societies, and most of them refused to accept colonialization by the French or the British. They fought with their organized armies and even produced their own weapons, using their metal smiths and gun powder experts. They also traded with the British and Spanish for weapons, because the Spanish and British came to purchase their captives and slaves which they sold to raise money for much needed supplies. They never knew that the slavery of the Europeans was so different from theirs, where the slaves had families, hunted with them and even served on their armies and gained their freedom.

Colonization in the allowed the Europeans to gain control of a large amount of lands throughout Africa; including the people, animals and other resources like lumber, iron, gold, bauxite, water, rice, nuts, berries, spices, cloth and later oil, as well as other discovered mineral like copper, etc. Through Colonialization they took control of many tribes and imported many of them to the coast and to the America's for slavery real cheap. This system made many of the European nations, traders and buyers very wealthy. This was the cycle in which Europe became one of the riches groups of nations in the world and was able to rebuild their countries into what they are today, the kingdoms, and the Papal society benefitted greatly; through the enslavement off of the enslavement of African nations and people. It also allowed the colonist to develop very wealthy plantations, farming industries, businesses and communities, cities and states in developing the North and South, Mexico and Canada as well. All of this was built on the back of slavery and the destruction of African peoples.

CHAPTER THREE

Colonialization and Colony development in America

The British, French, Spanish, Portuguese, Italians all came to the America's the British, Spanish and French all came to North America and developed settlements from Canada to Mexico, they disputed and fought over land, then agreed on particular lands for their colonialization, which developed into nations, states of nations and even cities. The French, Spanish, Portuguese and Italians developed colonies in South and Central America, as well as throughout the Caribbean, throughout Africa and it coast along with the British. For over three hundred years they fought and carved up North, South and Central America; as well as the Caribbean. During all this Africans were deported through all these lands and forced into slavery. They became new people with new languages and cultures. They mixed with the Spanish, Italians, Portuguese, French and British.

In North America slaves played a central role in developing and defending the country. Slaves were armed to help fight, hunt and capture Indian people and destroy their nations. When Africans came to North America they went through being auctioned off in Mississippi, Charleston, New Orleans, New York, and other places cities or towns. Then they were usually taken to places where they were broken so as to be easily dealt with by their white master's and mistresses. Many of the women were raped and the men beaten, so they understood who was in power, as well as who was the slave. Slavery was a difficult and ugly business; slaves had to be broken in. They were basically a usable item, which masters strived to get maximum use out of physically. Slave's humanity was taken by the whip, the gun, and the hanging tree. They knew this and knowing and obeying kept them alive, thinking the master was a nice guy got them buried and they knew it. Slaves hunted, captured or killed the Indians because it was their duty. They fought in the Revolutionary War and George Washington promised to free them but he didn't, even as the first American President. He rescinded the order and continued slavery and he ordered that all Blacks would be relieved of their guns, their military privilege and be returned to their masters. THAT WAS THEIR REWARD FOR HELPING TO DEFEND THE COLONIST LIBERTY AND HELP GAIN THEIR INDEPENDENCE. The colonists were brutal when it came to Blacks. They persecuted them and didn't give an inch when it came to freeing the slaves. Though George Washington and others said, they would reward the slaves with freedom for fighting the good fight, many giving their lives, other returning wounded, many with limps missing. They were returned to slavery and all of the Black soldiers weapons were removed from them because the Whites had realize their abilities to fight, especially with arms and they didn't want these men turning those weapons on them in the fight for their freedom.

Many of the Indian Nations treated the slaves better then the Americans did. This is why hundreds ran away and joined with the Indians, and fought against the settlers in many of their battles. Never the less, most slaves didn't run away, didn't participate in slave revolts, but fought in every war throughout America's history. Much of this wonderful history never got in American history used in our public, private and religious schools throughout the United States of America. This clearly was eliminated on purpose because the government didn't want Whites or Blacks to know the truth. Most Americans would said, you're lying if you'd told them thousand of Blacks died in the Revolutionary War, Civil War, and the War of 1812. Most Americans would say you're lying if you told them about Black Pilots fighting in WWI and WWII. The truth has been eliminated from the History books for a reason. The Government refused to document and distributes this history like they did the history of White soldiers, for one reason only they want Americans to know the history of Whites defending America but they don't want Blacks or Whites to know the history of Blacks defending America. An very few people will take the extra time and money to read Black history books to learn the facts. Later in the 1960's this history became a separate history called 'Black History' and students only learnt this stuff in Black History classes, which a few White students actually took, as well as many Black students didn't take Black studies classes either; they didn't think it was that important.

Let's reach back for a minute to understand something. An African Leader by the name of Samory Toure refused to allow the French to colonize his nation; he trained his army to produce their weapons; rifles and guns. He organized his military into units, artillery, infantry, scouts and those on horses. He built and brought small ships and boats to retrieve and move supplies throughout his country (area that now is part of Mali and Guinea). He is former Guinea President Senghor Toure Great Grandfather. He refused to submit or negotiate with the French and allow them to control his country, enslave his people. He never surrendered to the French and fought all of life against French colonialization. He did participate in selling slaves mostly through the tri-Sahara slave trade and then with the tri-Atlantic slave through the British or Spanish, trading war captives. Many African leaders sold war captives at first to the Europeans for weapons, food, cloth and other supplies. Then later many African leaders began trading their own people for European liquor, weapons, and other supplies. This lead to Europeans able to make deals that lead to Europe taking over Africa and controlling much of the land through African puppet governments and through direct rule using European ministers, developing embassies throughout the country. Africans throughout Africa fought off the French, Germans, Spanish, British, and Dutch who were coming feeling they had the right to colonize the land and usurp the resources in order to enrich their nations. Most of these nations were as poor as can be, the Kings and Queens were suffering, even the Papal government was suffering and needed an infuse of gold and silver, supplies of good food, cotton, and other stuff that could restore luxurious lifestyle and power. Whites in Europe was suffering, their out post in the Caribbean and North America was a dream come true, there nothing wonderful land and resources like animals, crops, trees, everywhere. They needed resources people to work for nothing, slaves and Africa have one of the largest resources for people with skills to farm, build, plow, and restore wealth to Europe and its people. That's the key word; they didn't care about Africa and its people. They only cared about Europe and its people. This attitude became part of the reality of the Colonist also as they struggled to build this new nation. The result was more important to them then African lives, communities and nations. Caucasian lives were more important to them and that's why they never looked back, never tried to reach a mediation with the Africans, tried to establish an honorable relationship with them, just as they never did with the Aboriginal people of the America's and the Caribbean.

After awhile, Europeans were governing most of Africa through direct and indirect (puppet governments) rule. They had militaries and forts in place, ship yards as well. They had police, courts, prisons and garrisons. They controlled slavery directly and were able to supply the America's with a constant supply of people until the United States broke with England and to get back at the United States England discontinued the slave trade under their control. This only slowed down the system because the colonist had already moved on. They continued to work with pirate slave dealers, the tri-Saharan slave traders and at slave breeders. Slavery wasn't slowing down in the least. America was independent from England so all its wealth now went towards its government, its people (accept the African people) and for development. by that time there were many breeding plantations continuingly producing and raising family less children into slaves as a business.

Breeding truly developed in the south and became one of its biggest businesses. They systemized breeding into a science; they counties of Mulatto and Octoroon men and women in places like New Orleans, or Mississippi to work at whore houses, on ferry boats for the rich, as dancers and performers, and at specialty clubs for White men. These Blacks could pass for white but they made good money for their owners and the towns they were in, even these slaves made good money and almost forgot they were slaves. On the big farms they utilized different types of Africans, such as Mandingoes, Fulani, and Wolof who were strong and good builders. The Ashanti were great clothes makers and weavers, as well as fishermen and farmers. The Africans from Gambia, Senegal, Mali and Guinea spoke Arabic and could read and write more then one language. Many were utilized to build and design houses, buildings, roads and carriages. Their was a lot of talent among the Africans, many had been sailors, fishermen, hunters, soldiers, in their homes some were princes and princesses, a king or queen was there also. They were broken in the America's raped, beaten, and worked so hard their bodies began to fall apart, dying from all types of illnesses. Slaves didn't have long lives usually, especially the field hands.

In the United States of America slaves were utilized in every aspect of the American economy as farmers, carpenters, brick layers, road and fort builders, scouts to hunt down Indians and runaway slaves, architects to design housing, soldiers during wars, workers on ships, office workers (especially cleaning offices in the south and north), garbage collectors, construction workers, sewing clothes, musicians at parties for the master, wagon drivers, husbandry workers, tending horses and other animals, clothes washers, factory workers in the south and north, gunsmith, ironsmith, horse trainers, etc. cooks, barbers, as well as inventors of many of the major inventions throughout America's history.

Whites truly benefitted from African slave labor, but no matter what the Africans did it was the master who benefitted from their work. Slaves were utilized in developing inventions but their masters got the financial and public benefit from their labor, invention and creation. Many owners would rent their slaves out and received the pay; although, some owners would allow slaves to work in order to make enough money to pay off their freedom. Usually if a slave was creative and invented something it was the master who got most of the benefit from the slaves ideas and work. There's a wonderful book called, "Black Inventors of America by McKinley Burt, Jr." . . . Every family in America should have a copy. It wasn't until the 18th and 19th Century that some of the inventions of Blacks went under their names, but Blacks were inventing throughout slavery. This documents that the negative ideas about people of color has no merit! During the Reconstruction period when slavery was over many Blacks went into politics becoming political leaders throughout the country. Many Black inventors were able to receive credit for their inventions before segregation and the black codes were established throughout the south and even many parts of the north. Blacks were again relegated to second class citizens and were segregated on city buses, trains, in restaurants, hotels, schools, universities, colleges, the military, in military bases, on jobs, in business and throughout America once again; segregation and Black codes became apart of the new history of America once again.

CHAPTER FOUR

Opening eyes in the Belly of the beast

My Grandmother was not an angry woman, she was really sweet but she died very sad, sitting on a stoop of a cement box called an apartment in South Carolina. It had come to this, sitting on the stoop of a building looking down on dirt with no grass, no flowers and no trees; sitting around people with no dreams and no hopes. 96 years of living around cows, horses, pigs, dogs and cats, trees and flowers everywhere, birds flying singing and dancing in the wind; picking herbs to sooth the throat, relaxing her legs on the stoop in the wind blowing smells of flowers.

There's a story about the American Indians and how they were villains; but what you would you do if someone came to your home, put you in the street, took your home and everything within it. They imprisoned you and your family because you were upset and fought for what you worked for all your life. My grandmother loss her home and died lonely, homeless and sad; like Geronimo, Cochise and other Indians throughout the America's.

The beast was the Whiteman who didn't have a conscience when it came to the Indian people or African people. Although, there was law, rights, the Constitution and Bill of Rights for whites but nothing for Indians and Africans. For those people of color there were reservations and plantations. Whites used the Buffalo soldiers as hunters of Indians, and they were wonderful in their job, they caught Geronimo and brought him in to die as a prisoner. A wonderful job for the oppressed to hunt another oppress person. That's how White America created American history using the African or the Indian to hunt and kill each other. Nevertheless, we stood at least "one sixtieth of the total Continental

Army in the Revolutionary War states, Major Donald L. Miller in "An Album of Black Americans in the Armed Forces". Every American should know this fact. I never read much about the contributions of Blacks in America until I met people like Malcolm X, Dr. Yusef Ben Jochannan, Professor Simmons, Professor Audrey Lorde, Playwright Ed Bullins, Amiri Baraka, and discovered black bookstores in Harlem. We are still being omitted in school history given a one month notation/mention called Black History . . . we need inclusion. Black History is American History. When the curriculum for public and private schools is revamped, including Nat Turner, Martin Luther King, Jr., Malcolm (El Hajj Malik El Shabazz) X., Harriet Tubman, ... make the history real tell the real story.

CHAPTER FIVE

Turning the Lie Around

It's wonderful today to watch television and see so many Black folk on television, on the movie screen, working as news casters, pro sports figures, doctors, lawyers, teachers, nurses, executives, soldiers private to generals, police captains, commissioners, commanders, airplane pilots, etc. it's truly a wonderful thing. Still we can't forget how we came this far African-Americans weren't always treated this good in America, and many Black folk have seem to forgot the heavy burden we've gone suffered.

We must save our youths minds, and tell the truth. Stop the white lies! White is not better then Black, Black is not better then White, no people are better then another. Patrick Henry was correct, "Give Me Liberty, or Give me Death" and so was Nat Turner, "I have done nothing I'm ashamed of. I'm fighting for my Freedom!" and so was Harriet Tubman, "You'll continue to freedom or you'll die right here". Black soldiers stood with George Washington tell the truth.

Race is something White folks developed for a particular reason in terms of goals and accomplishments. They were evolving and needed wealth, supplies, materials that would allow them to become a strong nation. The America's and the Caribbean would allow them to obtain the resources they needed and they also needed a cheap labor source, so this group of Nations that though connected by Christianity and the Pope decided to work together in sending Columbus on his journey to the East in search of goods that would add wealth, as well as much needed supplies like food, cloth, spices gold or silver. Instead Columbus discovered a whole new world, with people and source of food.

had worked together destroy Isof wiping any historical record of Islam in Europe. They wiped out Mosque, libraries, housing, schools, art, families, businesses, and architecture: rather buildings, roadways, gardens, hospitals, tapestry, books, and Islamic establishments. Muslims where killed, enslaved and became servants on farms and plantations that were placed in the hands of the Spanish. Caucasians began to establish a racial standard, to develop a society of the aristocracy and serfdom (the servants who worked for the Aristocracy) in order to develop a strong economic system to stabilize Europe and the colonialist economy. Racial nationality began to become a key factor in Europe and the colonies they set up in the Caribbean, and the America's. Europeans began to expand once they realized there was so much land and resources throughout the Caribbean and North America. Europeans began to expand across the Atlantic. The slavery of Africans were established throughout the colonies for one reason, to develop wealth and resources for Europe. Africans were treated cruelly and even many of the Indian Nations captured them and enslaved them. Whites abandoned the fields where they were forced to work as serfs, running away mixing in cities and running away where they could seek out land for themselves. This is how colonial cities developed throughout the Caribbean and in Colonial America. Slavery of Africans were instituted because whites were refusing to become servants and wished to own their land, farms and businesses. The serfs began to organize and enslave the Africans by force, forcing them to develop farms and plantations.

The British militia was also utilized to subdue the Africans who fought back throughout the Caribbean and North America. Many of the Africans developed their own settlements, towns and farms, some of these settlements in the Caribbean still exist. The European settlements and their militias grew stronger due to being supplied weapons by the European governments, who thought these European settlements were still beholding and supportive of the Aristocratic governments. Which in the beginning they were, even George Washington fought with the British in the beginning as a British General before he became a General for the Colonial army.

The colonialist worked for the welfare of the King and Queen of England, as well as was loyal to the Pope until England separated form the Rome Catholic Church and developed their own Christian church. The Colonialists paid taxes to England and fought with England against the Spanish. Their taxes as well as tobacco, cotton, vegetables, grains, and spices went to Europe as a form of subsidy to England. This system began in the Caribbean and transferred over when settlements moved across the Ocean to the America's.

When the colonialist began to develop settlements they came into direct conflict with many Indian Nations. Many of the African settlers helped in developing relationships with Amerindians, many of the African cultures were very similar to the Indian cultures. The Africans related easier to the indigenous cultures of the indigenous people, although many African settlements were attacked by Indians and many of their killed, put into slavery. Although, under of the Indian cultures the Africans learned the languages and traditions, inter-married with the Indians, as well as taught the Indians about weapons such as guns and rifles, building wooden houses and larger boat development. Through this relationship many Indian nations were able to confront the Europeans better. Many Africans became leaders in the Apache, Seminole, Black Foot, Cherokee, among others such as the Six Nations of the Mohawk. To this day many Indians are composed of many with African blood, throughout the United States of America, Mexico, Canada, the Caribbean, South America, and Central America, Australia and even in Hawaii. Africans travelled a lot to maintain their freedom, as well as to fight for their freedom.

Black people hatred for slavery forced them to join with the British to fight against the Colonialist in the American Revolution, with the colonialists against the British, with the Spanish and even with the Indians. Their major goal was to obtain their freedom. The Whites began to call Africans "Blacks", "Negroes", "Niggers-Lo life" and most all they were "barbarians" . . . An they began to right books stating the blacks were backward, lacking the ability to learn or speak properly, were evil, illiterate, backward, less then human, ugly, not religious, needed Caucasians to civilize them. By the time the American Revolution began Caucasians had completely developed chattel slavery throughout most of the thirteen colonies. Though, there were free Blacks, some had brought their freedom, many were born free, and others had ran away to freedom. Slavery in the USA was harsh, you could not marry. You had no rights over your own person or your children. You could be whipped, tar and feathered then burned to death, beaten to death or hung. You could be sold away from your family never see them again. Your wife and daughter could be raped by the master, any of his relatives or friends that he wished. If the master wanted mulatto babies he could force you to have his children, so he could sell them for more money then the darker children, unless the children were Mandingo, Fulani, Hausa, Watusi or Zulu which really rare. The Mandingo and Watusi were tall and strong and were used a lot as breeders or to built houses, roads and wagons. The Fulani and Hausa were good with horses, they knew how to care, breed and heal them when the horses were sick. The Zulu were from South Africa, a rare breed in America and they too were strong and made good breeders. The traders usually knew what breed the slaves were, or if they was just niggers, who meant those who were breed for so long that they had to history. The niggers worked in the field till they were of no more use, then they did any kind of labor until they died. Only a few owners, cared for their slaves and allowed them to socialize with each other, know their parents and live together in families. Although, that was really rare but in some states where the likes weren't as harsh as others the slaves grew up knowing there pappy and mother's. In places like Arkansas, Mississippi, Tennessee and parts of the Carolina and Georgia the slaves were treated real badly. Any Klan territory slavery was harsh, and many slaves were beaten and shot to death for looking harsh at the master. If looked at a white woman they were whipped, and many times hung and their balls cut right off. Trading was regular on breeding farms, where men and woman were constantly used mostly for breeding and they were sold or killed when they were of no more use. The pretty, big butt and real light ones were sold to prostitution whore houses where the women serviced men and women, making the owner very wealthy, especially with the hunters, cowboys, railroad workers, soldiers, and travelling businessmen. The prostitutes worked in salons, whore houses, cabaret houses even in mama and papa homes (small families with a few female slaves that they worked as prostitutes so they could make money to enlarge their farms.

Slavery was the source of the poor colonist enrichment, it was the slaves that worked from sun-up to sun-down growing crops, raising the animals, cooking and cleaning. It was the slaves who were rented out to the railroad to work alongside, the Indians and Chinese building the USA railroad system throughout America. It was slave labor that worked developing American cities, building houses, roads, streets, lamps and worked as firemen putting out fires in many early cities. Slave labor was used in almost every form but the master always got the money for renting the slaves out, accept the few whites that allowed slaves work out the farm to raise money to buy their freedom.

Read the history of Harriet Tubman, Sojourner Truth, Denmark Vesey, Martin Delaney, Nat Turner, Fredrick Douglass and Omar Ibn Said an African Enslaved in America who was an Senegalese trader and Qur'anic teacher. He wrote in Arabic and read the Qur'an but was forbidden to in North Carolina where he was enslaved. Africans were not an ignorant people, nor were they uneducated, non spiritual people. They came from kingdoms, empires, cities, states, education, civil governments, that existed even longer then the Roman and Greek empires. Many African Empires fought against the Romans, Greeks, Persians, Britain's, Arabs, Turks, and beat them, keeping them at bay from their nation. Egypt, Ethiopia, Cathrage, Sudan, Nubia, etc. were ancient Black nations, and there were many nations and kingdoms throughout Asia, Arabia and Africa of so-called Black peoples, which had flourishing kingdoms during and before the history of Caucasian ones. Many Caucasians, Romans, Greeks, Britain's, etc. were slaves captured in wars of Black nations. Hannibal was ruler of Cartrage, and led his army into Rome defeating its army, to revenge his father's death. Most of the rulers of Egypt for thousands of years were African long before Julius Caesar, Mark Anthony and the Greek Alexander the so-called Great ventured into Africa. Those statutes in Egypt and Nubia represent the African history of those beautiful people who developed, ruled, governed and maintained civilizations long before the Roman or Greek empires.

CHAPTER SIX

The Colonizers System of Racism

Christo Columbo wasn't a racist in that he hated black people, he basically set out to bring poor whites and imprisoned African-Muslims who ruled Spain for nearly seven hundred years, building universities, cities, civil government, hospitals, civic law, businesses and employment for the masses.

To the Caribbean to help the Europeans who re-conquered Spain develop these lands. He sought to utilize poor Europeans and the imprisoned Muslims to develop the Caribbean Island of Hispaniola, to produce vegetables, foods, grains, tobacco and nuts, etc. for Spain, Rome, Britain, Portugal and France. When he opened up the expansion of exploration into the Caribbean he led the way to the enslavement and death of millions of Indians and Africans over the next six centuries.

He was an explorer, merchant seaman and trader. His goal was to become wealthy and to provide the poor nations of Britain, Spain, France, Italy and Portugal with a source of wealth, which was very much needed. Nevertheless, by bringing these poor whites and imprisoned African Muslims to the Caribbean to work as serfs for a period of seven years he was opening the door to the destruction of millions of Indians and Africans.

Europe was really suffering, especially the Kingdom of King Ferdinand and Queen Isabella. They had just won the kingdom back but they were poor, they even lacked water to wash on a regular basis because the Europeans destroyed many of systems that the Muslims build, including the water systems. The city had to be rebuilt, and they lacked the money to rebuild. They wanted Columbo to travel to China and obtain spices, silver, gold, foods and materials to empower them. They were obtaining loans from the Pope who was spiritual leads of all the Christian states, as well as Britain and Portugal. Once Columbo would develop a relationship with leaders of China and open the door to trade Spain would be able to rebuild their kingdom.

Columbo did better than that by mistake. He discovered a whole new world full of fruits and vegetables which Europe lacked. By mistake he brought wealth and a new world of exploitation to Europe. The Indians were nice, they saved them from starving but were thanked by being overpowered and forced to work developing farms and plantations which they never did before. This didn't work out well for the Indians who weren't used to laboring in the hot sun farming all day, nor were they used to the whites diseases which affected, especially syphilis that near destroyed the people. They had no medicines to protect from the outbreak and hundreds died, many more later. This was the reason Columbus (really Colombo) decided to ask the Pope, King and Queen to allow him to bring over prisoners from the dungeons and the poor to work. Once this was approved and ships began to arrive with Muslims who were the first Africans brought to the Caribbean, they were captives from the Spanish Inquisition. They were from throughout North, Northwest and West Africa most of them were educated; spoke Arabic fluently, some were teachers, doctors, architects, etc. Most of the Europeans were simply the poor, prostitutes, beggars, criminals, etc. Nevertheless, all were given seven years of work, and they would be free to obtain there own land. This system worked well for awhile, the Africans and Caucasians worked together in the fields, although many of the Africans were able to utilize their professions to help heal the sick, design better housing, schools and farms. This was working out well and small towns developed. Many of the serfs were released and began to develop towns, farms, and businesses, including the Africans.

As word got out about the Caribbean, Portugal, Spain, Italy, France, Britain and even the Dutch began to send explorers. An eventually the coast of North America was being explored and discovered. An more Indian nations were also discovered, which caused internal conflicts as the explorers, began to take over land, infringe on the Indians hunting, living and burial grounds. They also began to explore the Caribbean more and discover more land, which they followed into South and Central America. Europeans were now infringing upon lands of the Indians, and lead to many wars, and much death. The Caribbean, South, Central and

North America became a field of death for the indigenous people. The Whites began to arrive in ships with armies, explorers, civilians whose aim was to obtain land and create a better life for them and they didn't worry about what happened to the indigenous people.

Millions of the Indigenous people perished, were evacuated from their homes, and became slaves, prostitutes and servants for the explorers and settlers. Indian lands were taken, Indians removed to reservations and interim camps. Slowly the Indigenous people were wiped out and the Caribbean, North, Central and South America became European nations. As the Spanish, French, Italian, English and Portuguese took of them.

Even in these lands, the Whites didn't want to slave in the fields, so they too looked toward Africa and now the explorers began traveling their and ripping into the indigenous people there. This time for slaves and then for gold, diamonds, bauxite, copper, lumber, spices, and other minerals, came the explorers. They were surprised of the Africans, who had civilized and organized Empires, Nations, Cities, States, Religions, Armies, Navies, and many had large ships, gunpowder and rifles.

Many of the Africans had been dealing with the Saharan Slave trade, as well as the Tri-Atlantic Slave trade and were obtaining rifles, guns and ammunition for their slaves. Many of the Kingdoms were fortified and wouldn't bundle to European challenge of warfare and conquering them. Europeans began to trade on the coast of Africa, with African and Arab traders. The African and Arab traders brought their brought captives from the interior to the coast and sold these people to the European traders. Then the European traders would load the belly of the ship with human cargo, bagged and tagged like all other cargo, stacked and loaded like bundles of wood or cloth. In these long travels across the Atlantic ocean hundreds of people who died or got sick were thrown overbroad to the sharks.

Europe wanted a cheaper product, so they send more equipped military along with the slave traders, so they could trade directly with the Kings, chiefs, warlords, Heads of State, and Khalifahs (Islamic heads of State). Most of the European military leaders wanted to take over rule of these African nations and rule by indirect rule, supplying the leader with alcohol, European cloth, weapons, and money. While taking over direct rule of his country, and allowing for slavery of his people, as well as the withdrawal of many of his people as slaves, plus minerals, lumber, etc. Some rulers would accept the agreement because they were afraid to fight, but many of Africa's leadership refused and internal war with in lasted for over three centuries. Many of these nations that fought the Europeans continued also to supply slaves through direct and indirect trade, but refuse to allow the European to take over direct control of their Nation, Empire or Tribe. People like the Mahdi in the Sudan, Samori Toure in Northwest Africa, Chaka Zulu in South Africa fought with well trained militaries and kept the French and British from conquering them for years.

CHAPTER SEVEN

They came with Fire Power & the Bible

Europe came for only one thing to obtain wealth, to obtain minerals, spices, lumber, people, animals, oil, and other materials that allow them to enrich their governments, the rich, and their businesses. Slavery, colonialism and imperialization was only for one thing to allow first for poor European Kingdoms to become wealthy, second for those kingdoms to become politically stronger with more developed army, and thirdly for these Kingdoms to become a world power. This happened for the slave trading and colonizing states of England, France, Germany, Britain, Spain, Portugal, Belgium, Italy and Holland. All of them became powerful, wealthy and independent due to the slave trade, and colonialism. All of these nations including the United States of America was subsidized and build off of the blood and work of Indians and especially Africans forced into slavery. Whites build their nation and wealth off of the labor, pain and death of Africans (Blacks, African-Americans, Hispanic-Americans, Afro-French-Americans) . . . ..
Slaves got there language from their masta, whatever the masta spoke the slave spoke. The slave wasn't allowed to speak and an African, or Amharic or Arabic—Coptic language. We Spanish, French, Portuguese, English, Dutch, Russian, etc speaking Black folk speak the masta tonque! Understand.

Masta came with fire power to take us from our homes and sorry greedy Kings, Tribal leaders, Khalifs, etc stole and sole us for peaces of gold or silver, alcohol, goats, boats, weapons, etc. The Europeans came with Guns and the Bible. The Arabs came with guns and the Qur'an. Nevertheless, we were stole, brought and taken from our home and sold.

Which is how all of the people with color landed in these European nations. An why most of us are still in dramatic shock because we haven't yet realized that its time we stop playing around and study, read, learn, save and stop spending and wasting our hard earned funds on all these European toys, gadgets sold and taking our hard earned money, so we have nothing to improve our families life. They gave us gadgets for our people, land, minerals, bodies and most of all our minds: and they are still always selling newer and better gadgets, even drugs, cigarettes, bad food and alcohol. We basically are still slaves, fighting each other over nonsense and killing each other nonsense. Marrying and breaking up over nonsense that if we sat and thought about we could work through it.

When the Spanish, French and British came to Africa they realized that Africa was not going to as easy to colonize as the Caribbean and the America's. They were confronted with kingdoms, nations, empires and tribes of all types and sizes. Who didn't wish to meet, negotiate or meet the Europeans? Slaves were brought from European, Arab and African slave traders. Who met the traders along the coast of Africa, many dared to travel into the interior and met with organize African armies, many of which to their surprise rode horses and had weapons. Africans even had boats and ships, so in the beginning Europeans had a difficult time venturing into the interior of Africa and negotiated agreements with coastal slave traders, who were already dealing with the trans-Saharan slave trade and was willing to expand their trade with the Europeans for weapons; especially rifles, knives, and such. This wasn't pleasing to the Europeans who had hardly any problems in the Indians in the America's because of their weapons and horses. Here many of the Africans had horses and weapons, some nations even produced their own weapons. They weren't negotiating with the Whites for their people or for land. Africans in North and North West Africa, the Sudan had already confronted the French in battle. In West and East Africa they were confronting Britain and later the Belgium's, as well as the Spanish. In the fifteenth century Africans had well developed nations and city—states, with schools, universities, housing, paved streets, etc. When confronted with European arrogance and demands for taking over rule of their country, land and people many African people decided to go to war. Although, many African leaders sold out their people for gold trinkets, alcohol, rifles and the right to continue as leaders under European political ministers, Christian ministers to teach them Christianity and indirect rule.

With this Africans began, setting up ministries in Africa, and were able to develop ministries in North, South and West Africa, the French and Spanish coming through North Africa into Morocco, Mauritania, Tunisia, Algeria, Libya, then into Egypt, although there were constant internal battles with Islamic believers throughout this region, even in the Songhai Empire, and Timbuktu and among the Hausa, Fulani, Yoruba, in West Africa. Samori Toure let a long battle against the French in the area called Guinea today. He developed a strong military, even manufactured is own rifles and guns, as well as brought weapons from the Spanish and English slave traders, as well as from Arab traders in the Trans-Saharan Slave trade which he continued to sell his African captives from other tribes to. Africa had a slave trade going back to ancient times in Europe with Rome, Greece, Spain, Britain and France. It wasn't the slave trade that bothered Africans, but the fact that Europeans were coming into Africa to take control of the land and its people. This time they came with fire and war, and wished to give Africans their white God Jesus.

CHAPTER EIGHT

They came to Conquer the World . . .

From the Conquering of the New World; North, South and Central America and well as the Caribbean they march straight across the sea to Africa to obtain more subjects. This time the slaves would have no rights at all, nothing like the slaves of Ancient Rome, Greece, Persia and Egypt who could marry, win their freedom through battle, and service to the Emperors or Master. This new slavery was new, it was based solely upon the complexion of the skin and it was for life, generational for the entire continuous family. There was no freedom, never for sons or daughters. Slavery as an institution became final, the slaves were no longer Human being but cattle, to be brought and sold, killed, beaten, and reproduced at the "masters will". It was called chattel slavery, because the Blacks were no longer considered human beings, but animals like cattle, to be branded, beaten, fed, and treated like animals. The "whites" went about trying to justify this system by writing books that showed that Blacks were biologically different then whites, inferior intellectually and physically then whites.

The trouble with this nonsense was African Kingdoms still existed and weren't surrendering and giving up their land like the Indians in parts of North, South and Central America. The Africans didn't just have spears, like the movies presented and didn't just wear feathers and head gear with feathers, nor did they all wear clothes of skin. Africans were weaving cotton and other fabrics, sewing cloth into elaborate dresses, gowns, robes, pants and skirts. Were designing hats, scarf's, and producing jewelry for Kings and Queens, rode on horses, as well as designing and building all types of housing and architecture, from mud, clay, wood and cement. They had city-states like Egypt, Ethiopia, Canaan and the home of Hannibal the great Carthage (who fought Rome and ruled it). Both Rome and Carthage had slaves taken as prisoners of war living in their societies, also women who they mated with and had children with. Racism wasn't a part of their reason for their wars and struggles but a matter of who will rule each other. These struggles continued for years and through many internal battles. Just as the Persians, fought the Romans and Greeks to see who would rule who and become the leaders of their world. Africans were great warriors like Samori Toure, Hannibal the great, Chaka Zulu, Askia Muhammad Toure, and the Mahdi in the Sudan. "In the Colonial Reader: Colonial Africa by Wilfred Carley and Marin Kilson", there is a statement "not only did all European powers participating in the scramble for Africa in the 18th Century confront some armed resistance from the African traditional rulers, but in some cases, the resistance was substantial and of some duration." Africans had basically held European colonialization down from the fifth teen century to the 19th century. African states were well organized into states, confederacies, and nations and responded to European nations imposing force to usurp their nations with war an intense battle, pushing many European nations toward the coast. "This was markedly so in the wars between the British and the Ashanti Kingdom in the nineteenth century. The British began to assert authority over trade, especially the slave trade, on the Gold Coast (now Ghana) in the early nineteenth century, and met fierce resistance from the well-organized Ashanti Confederacy which had established wide influence in the slave trading to the Western Hemisphere in the 18th and 19th century" is stated on the first page of the introduction of the book of Wilfred Carley and Martin Kilson. Africans refused to give up their fight for freedom even against the big guns of Europe.

The slave trade was extremely important to Europe because it would allow them to capitalize off of human bondage. Only by enslaving people of color would these Europeans fell superior in their desire to again become wealthy and powerful. By creating a racial based system of slavery, human exploitation and bondage; humans felt truly powerful and a new world power. They began to document this atrocity by falsifying religious, scientific and historical records. Lying about the quality of African peoples historical existence in religion, science, education, politics and social living. They rewrote the historical record, making Africans an inferior people throughout history and in many cases non-existent in the historical record. Replacing Caucasians instead of people of color in Egypt, Ethiopia, Europe, Asia, Indonesia, the Caribbean, and throughout the America's as the developers of culture, science, the arts, cities and nations. They even eliminated people of color in their relationship to Buddha, Krishna, Muhammad, Jesus, and all the Prophets of Judaism, Islam and Christianity.

They fortified these lies in most of the historical records, based on books that most of us studied and read in school.

From the fifteen century Africans fought for over four hundred years against Europeans trying to usurp their freedom, through exploration, wars and battles, trying to wipe out African culture (polytheism, Islam, and African traditional forms of Christianity and Judaism. For four hundred years Europeans enslaved Africans; kidnapping and bringing them across the Atlantic developing the Tri-Atlantic Slave Trade from Africa to Europe, to the Caribbean, then to North, South and Central America. In the later eighteenth century Europe banned Slavery, basically to get back at the colonialist in the Caribbean and the America's. Slavery continued until after the Civil War in around 1869.

CHAPTER NINE

The development of America

The Dutch arrived in North America in around 1619 in a British man of war ship and Africans who were considered slaves were aboard. It was during this period that Europeans began arriving and bringing Moors from Europe who were the captives from the Spanish Inquisition. Having over five hundred years of ruling Spain the Islamic control was overthrown and King Ferdinand and Queen Isabella gained control of Spain. They begin to seen ships to North America about fifteen to thirty years after these new lands were discovered.

Most of these Africans were Muslim and had many skills such as farming, ship building, and carpentry, navigation of ships, writing and reading Arabic, Spanish and English. As workers they would come in handy in developing this land, especially in building homes, barns, stables and farming. As other Africans caught in Africa from its many tribes, kingdoms and villages; these Moors would come in Handy in breaking them in. The came and began to develop settlements but have to be careful because the Indians constantly harass and kill some of the settlers with their arrows and knifes if they get close enough.

The Moors are good fighters, hunters, scouts and good in building homes. They are used by the Europeans but are treated like companions at first because they are very skilled. They help fight off the Indians especially after some of the early settlers are killed by the Indians. As more and more ships arrive, the Moors are used as scouts and they help in developing the land and planting crops. When more Africans arrive they are put to work clearing the land, helping with building forts and housing, including slave quarters. More ships arrive from overseas, filled with supplies, rifles and guns, African slaves, as well as horses. With the guns and horses they can keep more control of the Indians and the Africans as well.

The Europeans capture Indian woman and mate with them, even have babies by them because there are few women among the settlers at first. Later ships arrive with Africans including their women, and many European women who are looking for husbands to start their new lives with. With the years more and more settlements develop and French and Spanish vessels arrive with settlers also. The French begin to trade with the Indians and introduce them to the horses and teach them how to use the rifles, as they trade for skins, buffalo meat and seeds to grow the corn and other stuff they've introduced to the settlers.

Many of the settlers have become friendly with some of the Indians and they trade with each other for supplies. Many of the Indians are curious about the Africans, and some of the Africans have disappeared into the woods and have set up settlements, others have befriended the Indians and have become friendly with them. Some slaves have started to run away and have become apart of the Indian tribe. The Europeans have become tougher and stricter on the African slaves. They keep the slaves now separate from Europeans with overseers watching them, along with the dogs that are on patrol. Many settlers have developed small plantations and have begun raising children. The slaves too have begun having children. These settlements continue to go and begin to take lands that were once Indian land. This causes problems with the Indians and battles ensue.

The settlements develop into colonies and the colonies into towns. Slowly cities begin to develop, with farms, towns, ranches, settlements, and saloons. The slave quarters develop larger and larger, especially in the plantations and ranches. The larger farms usually have as many as ten slaves and the small farms at least two or three. The English settlements have grown large and the King has begun taxing his people.

Laws have been established to keep the slaves and settlers in check. No slave can have an African or Islamic name, wear African clothing or speak African languages and deftly not practice any African religions. The Europeans wished to rid the Africans of any remembrance of any semblance of their African heritage. They wish rip their African culture from them. Those caught speaking African languages were beaten and the masters began to give every slave a name all the women and men got English names.

Many slaves ran away into the woods in order maintain their culture but those caught were beaten with whips, a few were hung to make a point and others were send to work in the woods to cut trees or to the docks to build ships, and the masters received some payment for their labor. Women were beaten also but the men got beaten with a hard leather belt or a whip, only women continued to cause trouble got beaten like the men. Master didn't want them not to be able to have babies, for babies guaranteed more bodies for the farm and plantations.

In Africa at around the same period around the British were still working its slave routes, negotiating with the Ashanti's in Ghana and the Yoruba in Benin and Nigeria to by slaves, many of the chiefs refused to sell their people, although they would sell their slaves and captives from other tribes. Many of the chiefs were a little worried about these people coming into their country looking to buy their people. Around this people Africans were organized into nations with Kings and Queens similar to Europe and very organized states with armies, scouts and farms, craft societies, and priest. They had slavery but their slaves moved around in the community and worked among the people, although some were sacrificed to the gods. They were seldom beaten like in Britain and the America's. Many of the slaves became great warriors and inter-married in the tribe. The chiefs felt slavery among these whites was similar to their own. They offered coins, traded liquor, weapons and sometimes horses similar but bigger then the ones the Arabs brought to trade. Horses had been important to the Yoruba and Hausa peoples, their horsemen were known for their speed and abilities in warfare, hunting and racing. They liked trading with the Arabs who came regularly bringing exotic spices, garments of silk, knives, daggers and now rifles for the soldiers and boats for the fishermen. The Arabs were also looking to buy slaves for their trading through Africa and along the Sahara.

The slave trade was big throughout Africa and Arabia, there were trading markets along the coast, within many villages with the Kings and their traders. Yet, as the European came to these lands he was always looking to purchase land, even forest area, as well as many people that the Africans were willing to trade, said he needed servants in his land. He came with these giant boats on the coast and many of them would raid the villages near the coast and drag as many people as they could. Around the coast of Africa there were small caves and dense trees where the monkeys and other animals rest and played away from the sun. He began to use these areas as holding areas for their captives until they got them onto the ships. There were many scrimmages among Africans and the Europeans and their slave catchers. Many bodies littered the Atlantic shores since these people arrived. From the 1600's until the early 20ᵗʰ century Europeans invaded Africa to obtain slaves through the early 1800's, after to colonize Africa in order to rule it through direct and indirect governing, so as to drain the resources of gold, silver, bauxite, copper, diamonds, lumber, oil, spices, animal hides and fur, exotic foods that only grew there and herbs that were used for medicines, as well as fish.

Europe was a very poor nation in the 1500's and they sources for food, spices, cloth, laborers, lumber, precious jewels, etc which they were lacking. They sought out Asia and Africa as their main source for those supplies, using their large 'Man of War ships' adventurous sailors who didn't have any employment at home, going to sea was full of adventure, exciting women, travel, and good pay. European sailors begin to travel the sea's pioneering and seeking out wealth, slavery was one the richest sources from the 16ᵗʰ century until the 20ᵗʰ century for many seafaring pirates, soldiers and businessmen of Europe and later the America's.

CHAPTER TEN

Developing Europe & America on the Bodies of Africa

Spain was poor in 1492 King Ferdinand and Queen Isabella came to the throne poor, with little money, no gold or diamonds and absolutely little resources to build the nation they just re-claimed from the Muslims. An they were stupid they destroyed have the country in order to wipe out the history of nearly six hundred years of rule by the Moorish Muslims. They had building, libraries, schools and universities destroyed. The torn down the hospital, gardens, tapestry, mosque and imprisoned any of the rich Moors that weren't able to retreat in to Morocco. They took all of their gold and silver but it wasn't enough to rebuild what they torn down. They reached out to the Pope, Britain, Portugal, and France for financial assistance. As a last resort they decided to ship a few ships on an excursion to the east to obtain goods that will allow the rebuilding of Spain. Thus began the voyages of Christofo Columbo (the man knows as Christopher Columbus. His six voyages were to the Caribbean for he never reached America. His journey was to go to the East, but he landed in the Caribbean, after in got caught in the Caribbean currents and almost perished. The excitement began when he met the aboriginal peoples who had never seen Caucasians before, but saved him and his crews life, giving them water and food. Columbo thanked them by usurping land, starting a farm and forcing the Indians to work it; which caused much personal hardship for them. The also began to obtain diseases from the sailors when they had sexual relations with the Indian women. The Indians were to fight off these illnesses because they had no immunity to them, and this caused problems between the Indians and the Spanish. Christofo Columbo also kidnap some Indians and took them to Spain to show them off to the King and Queen, along with the new foods, spices, animal skins and plants, especially tobacco for smoking.

The King and Queen were very excited, especially with tobacco, foods and Indians. They wanted to expand the amount of ships to this world, including more ships and sailors, as well as workers including some of the Africans Moors to help establish a small colony on these Islands. This was the beginning of the colonization of the Caribbean not America. That occurred in 1619 when the Dutch landed in the America's and introduced slaves. Although in the book, "The Black Frontiersmen by J. Norman Heard" It is certain that slaves were introduced in this hemisphere by the Spanish Ships less then years after its discovery. Estevanico a Moor who sailed from Cuba with the Narvaez expedition in 1528, was cast away on the coast of Texas coast, and made his way across deserts and mountains to the Pacific coast of Mexico. Later Estevanico discovered Arizona and entered New Mexico".

Christopher Columbus had six voyages to the Caribbean on the Island of Hispaniola which was the Island that houses the Republic of Haiti and the Dominican Republic today. Haiti began the first Independent Black Nation in the Western Hemisphere and T'oussaint L'Overture was its first President. He developed plantations on Hispaniola and during his voyages brought African captives from the Spanish prisons to become the first slaves in the Western Hemisphere. From Hispaniola the Spanish sailed down the coast and discovered North America, Columbus wasn't part of this voyage.

The relationship of the White men and the Indians were very difficult because the whites saw the Indians as dangerous and also because the whites objectives were one taking over the Indians land exterminating them. Only when they realized that this Indians weren't going to be exterminated or moved to other areas that easy, the whites began to talk about treaties, which they always changed to suit themselves not the Indians. As more and more whites heard about the America's and the Caribbean, wanted the lands for themselves even at the expense of eliminating the Indians all together. This attitude caused direct conflict with the Indian nations throughout America, and believe me there were many developed Indian nations. There were groups of Indian people that formed a collective like the six nations of the Mohawk, etc. The American Indians didn't surrender easily.

CHAPTER ELEVEN

White expansion and human destruction

If you read or research you'll find out that when whites expanded blacks and Indians died. Blacks were made into slaves for the white man. While Indians were pushed off of their lands, confined to reservations which was really prisons, buffalo and other food sources taken away, culture taken away, men murdered and women dying alone; white America expanded their lands, making larger plantations, cities, states and community constantly being developed on the bodies of Africans and Native Americans. White expansion, Black and Indian death that's the history of the United States of America, as well as Britain, France, Portugal, Spain Holland, Canada and Mexico. All build on the bodies of the Red and Black peoples. As every city grew more Indians were removed from their lands, more of them died or were killed; and yes more Blacks were enslaved and forced to work to build this great nation. It was built on the backs and bodies of Black and Red People. No reparations, No thank you, no Historical Documentation to honor the work done.

Today, as part Indian (I have Caucasian (maternal grandfather), Indian (paternal grandmother) African Maternal grandmother and paternal grandfather)) African and Indian I share the truth, so other people can realize that its time to stop the racism and bigotry. We all know how Obama became President folks all over this nation decided it was time for a change; Medgar Evers, President John F. Kennedy, Martin Luther King, Jr., four little girls in Selma praying in the church, Malcolm X, thousands of Black soldiers who fought and never got their freedom, millions of Black slaves who never got their freedom, millions of Indians who lose their lands, their families and their lives . . . Marcus Garvey, Nat

Turner, Denmark Vesey, Harriet Tubman, Rosa Parks, Sojourner Truth, Paul Robeson, Betty Shabazz, Geronimo, Cochise, Patrice Lumumba, Elijah Muhammad, Clara Muhammad, Fannie Lou Hamer, Matulu Shakur, and millions more imprison, died on reservations, died on plantations, died in wars but never got their freedom, died marching in the south for equal right, justice and liberty . . . . I love my brothers and sisters throughout the United States of America and on the United Indian Nations who are standing up for justice. Justice is when racism dies and true democracy shines . . . We can't bring back the dead but we can push racism out in the Senate, in the Congress, in the Assemblies and Senates throughout ever state in this nation, destroy racism and hatred in the streets, Churches, Mosque, Jewish Temples, schools, homes, institutions and nations . . . Obama won because America needed a change. People wanted to make a statement this a country ruled by only White men, but a Nation for all the People, of every nationality, religion, gender . . . as Mr. King said, "Let Freedom Ring"

White Expansion Human Destruction, no matter who you are, you're human and Caucasians are no different really between black and white. Both are prime colors, you can't imitate them, they are pure, you are pure and so are all of us. In Chinese philosophy yin and yang can become the other, they balance each other. We all balance each other gay and straight, girl and boy, black and white, red is black and white is yellow, each is each other . . . Caucasian men forgot that and only wanted power. They wanted to rule the world, become the big dog and they lose their balance. Blacks tried to show you, by fighting in every war even though they were slaves. The Indians saved you when you were weak and dying feed Columbus and the Pilgrims, then you got your strength and begin to enslave them, take the lands, slavery didn't work so you put them in reservations and enslaved the Blacks. You destroyed two people and hundreds of nation just to build your nations. You wiped out hundreds of millions of people for over six centuries to empower yourselves (too much yang and you become yin, there's imbalance and everything falls apart, you become very sick. Lincoln tried to balance the confusion but you killed him. He saw the light but like George did want to really take a change. He should've just step up there and said all slaves are free as of today. Kennedy hesitated also, didn't want shake things up too much. Martin didn't hesitate he said Black and White must walk hand and hand . . . The founding fathers thought that whites would probably revolt if they let the slaves go free but they would've saved four hundred years of murder, exploitation and confusion. Today, many of those rich white men still don't want blacks around even if they got money, but they don't realize they got blood money. Money made on the persecution and murder of black, white and red people; with yellow and beige mixed in. Its time to stop the murdering, time to let the slaves go free; today the rich white men are producing heroin and cocaine; along with the crazy Muslims in Afghanistan and Pakistan who won't let their wives or daughters go to and the Columbians. They're selling the drugs to the brothers in the white, black, Spanish hoods to keep the slaves out of mind and out of sight.

The whites were never hiding although they were lying. They told black men when the bullets were flying and they didn't have enough bodies on the field that they would free us. They began the lie when the Indians were kicking their behind. They called on the slaves to join forces with them, they gave us guns, although mostly broken one with not enough bullets but we made it work and we fought and many blacks died in every war, check the records. We started fighting when we came off the ship in shackles and the Indians were throwing spears, the white hid behind while the African ran towards the Indians and got a whole lot of arrows in his body. In every war after that we ran toward the enemy and have been running that way since, we want equality, justice, freedom and the opportunity to exercise our ability.

We fought in every war, from arrival on the shores of the Caribbean, to the landing on America with the Spanish, French and British. We fought in battles before the American Revolution, War of 1812 and the Civil War, as well as every war after, they refuse to allow into the military schools to learn to be officers but that didn't stop us, they wouldn't allow us to be sailor, so we stole the enemies ships and brought it home, then they let us on the sea. We learnt to fly in Tuskegee and flew in France with the French when our own country would not allow us to fly. We learnt to read plans, fly, drive, shoot, dive in the seas, operate all types of ships even, fly in the air, we learnt from the years of 1700 until the 2000's and we still growing.

Look up in the history books, take your mind out of racism and bigotry, tap your mind into truth and consciousness and realize, we're all basically the same. George Washington realized this but when the war was over he to folded and forced those black men who survived the war to be thrown back into the pit of slavery. General Andrew Jackson who became the 7th President of the USA; in 1814 made a call for Black men to join him in the defense of New Orleans and many blacks showed up to fight. These men were able to deter the British and help drive them back, that General Jackson was honored to fight with them. He was angered when he was suggested that they receive less pay then the whites, but he didn't stop them from being forced back into slavery when the war was over. Major Donald L. Miller, "An Album of Black Americans: In the Armed Forces" documents much of the history of Blacks in the Military, a must read book.

Throughout America's history Black men stood up and went to fight in wars, but America didn't respond in kind. They forced the Black men who fought in wars to defend this country back into slavery. They didn't see these Black men as human beings and they didn't give them justice for their commitment to the USA, not as slaves but free men. America's Great Presidents like George Washington, John Adams, Thomas Jefferson, James Madison, John Monroe, John Quincy Adams, and Andrew Jackson all great Presidents did absolutely nothing. They did nothing also when the Constitution and Bill of Rights was developed. These great men had slaves and plantations; they made a lot of their money off of the labor of slaves. They couldn't stand up against slavery because most of these great had slaves. Thomas Jefferson lived with a slave woman after his wife Martha passed. The slave woman was his wife's half sister, one of the women his wife father had sex and a child with (this was something that white men did regularly seduce their slaves). There were too many benefits for white men that they maintained slavery for over two hundred years because of the cheap labor, sexual encounters with slaves and feeling of power over blacks made them seem very powerful.

CHAPTER TWELVE

The trek towards freedom

The American Revolution was a dream and a desire for the colonialist who desired to run a nation. General George Washington had formerly been a General in the British military but desired to organize a professional army, not just a militia. He travelled throughout the colonies organizing and motivating the people, especially the men to prepare for war. He knew the British would hear nothing of giving the colonies their independence without a fight. He knew that once they found out the colonies were organizing they would send their army and man of war ship loaded to the brim with men, horses, rifles and canons. He knew the British abilities because he fought alongside General Braddock during the French and Indian War in 1755. During that war they had utilized Black men as scouts, engineers and foot soldiers, as recorded by, Major Donald L. Miller in his book, An Album of Black Americans in the Armed Forces. George Washington confronted the patriots and let them know to prepare for war. By early 1770, British troops were being station on these shores and were confronted by patriots, one a black man Crispus Attucks was the first man to fall dead from the British guns.

Major Donald L. Miller states, "that over five thousand black men, one sixtieth of the total Continental Army' fought in the Revolutionary War. He further states, free Black men citizens joined white minutemen in defending Lexington and Concord in April 1775." History records that George Washington asked the Continental Congress to reject all Blacks enlistment into the Army also states in his book. The British were more then happy to letting Black men join their army and offered them freedom. Once Washington and other's learnt of the British

Dunmore Proclamation they offered slaves freedom if they fought for the colonialist, nevertheless at the end of the war George Washington and the colonist didn't keep their word but forced the soldiers back into slavery, Major Miller clarifies in his book.

George Washington who becomes America's first President as well as one of the founding fathers of the new American Nation, wasn't going to be one of the enlighten Americans to truly free the slaves.

Blacks fought throughout the American Revolution and participated as foot soldiers, the cavalry, spies and scouts, crossed the Delaware with George Washington and were each of the army brigades of George Washington's army, Miller states. Blacks had their own regiments and commanders, one was called, "the Bucks of America" from Massachusetts, there were others in places like Rhode Island and Connecticut. Which fought in major battles, and others fought in White Plains, Bennington, Red Bank, Trenton, and Princeton. Miller states, "they fought with Washington at Valley Forge and aided in the defeat of Cornwallis at Yorktown". "An Act of Congress in 1792 restricted service in the militia to "able bodied white men." White men in America had a habit of using Black men to assist them in wars promising them freedom then returning them to slavery once the wars were over. During periods when slavery were over in the 19th and 20th centuries segregation and racism continued throughout the society, in the job market, schools, colleges and universities, housing, and throughout the broadcasting and movie industries.

White men wanted to contain Black men and limited their opportunities because they wanted to control every market and opportunities for themselves. Black helped to build and develop this nation, usually on the short order basis, helping out when the need was there, then dropped once the job was done. In civilian times, whites controlled the docks, carpentry, the building industry, electrical and engineering industries, education, medicine, housing development, transportation, movie, radio, publications, music, police and fire departments, FBI, CIA, and even the underworld crime (yes the white criminals didn't want competition of black criminals) racism and bigotry existed even among the criminals.

In 1864 General Sherman's forces devastated the Confederate forces during its march through Richmond, the capital of the Confederates which fell within six months. Few people know that black soldiers were the first to enter and "thirteen of them were awarded the Congressional

Medal of Honor after the war for their charge on the Confederacy at New Market Heights outside of Richmond." This led to the fall of Richmond and the surrender of General Lee to General Grant at Appomattox. Miller states, "Over 186,000 black soldiers were serving in the Union Army during the Civil War."

The truth is better than fiction which has been part of the story in most of our history books. In the 1960's during the Black Power Movement those of us educators were pushing for inclusion of the truth of Blacks in history in the curriculum of Public schools in New York City. We argued at board hears but the school board refused, so some us Black educators began to develop Black Independent schools and begin to educate Black and Hispanic students about true history. The Independent School system lasted nearly twenty years educating thousands of youth that went on to the best universities. We also developed the Black Student Union which organized Black college and university students. These programs created many Black professionals today who think out of the box, professors, doctors, architects, lawyers, etc. Many of us pioneers sacrificed better salaries, jobs and other benefits to educate Black youth, who weren't going to be dead heads, filled with a white based education. Although, we never taught the children just about Blacks, our historical curriculum was one of historical truth about humanity, out students learnt the truth and gained a humane perspective. By doing this we freed our children from a racist perspective, and example is my daughter who fell in love with a Caucasian and had three wonderful children. A race based education causes bigotry and racism to develop, that is what happens in the American school system. Due to the racial based education of the Public school system. You see Blacks weren't fighting to be separated from whites; they fought to a complete part of the American society. They wanted to live anywhere they could afford. They wanted jobs, careers, housing, peace, happiness, families, and most of all they wanted freedom to live out of bondage. Black Independent schools wasn't a racist move, as many Black and White educators suggested but a movement to force the government change their system of education. Many charter schools are doing what we started in the 80's and I want to say what is happening among the American Indian nations as well today. Today, the Indian communities are changing the books retelling the historical story. They are showing their children not to accept the White mans version of history. Fredrick Douglass, Harriet Tubman, Geronimo and Cochise tried to reason with the White's to give their people justice and inclusion. But the white eye's as the Indians called the whites didn't want to listen, they wanted all the good lands for themselves and the only thing the Indians and Africans were good for was laboring for them, or lying dead in graves. That's the true history of America, power and land hungry whites who threw off their oppressor to become oppressors themselves. All those White President's and founding fathers were oppressors of the 19th Century and most of the 20th century, If that isn't then why was their segregation and black codes, hanging, racial based employment called discrimination. Why did Americans Blacks, Whites, Indians and others march throughout the south and north for human and civil rights laws to be passed? Why did so many people have die, get beaten, water hosed, arrested and further more WHY didn't those Great Men like Washington who knew first hand the fact that Black fought and died for this Countries freedom. How dare he turn his back on their freedom and say he cared about 'freedom for all'. Who was that all only Whites! The trek for freedom for White women was difficult also and when we look at the Freedom Train, we see hundreds of White women and some men running the 'Underground Railroad'. WE see our beloved Washington, the Adams brothers, Jefferson and others not standing up for real justice but only for White Men. White women wasn't included in the Justice our Founding talked about,

Fredrick Douglass and Harriet Turner worked with abolishers who speaking out against slavery, and participated in promoting freedom for slaves, opportunities, education, women's rights, and equality throughout the American society. Susan B. Anthony worked with them and also developed a women's organization to obtain rights for women. They all worked to overall change America, its politics and social structure. Which came to naught because racism and sexism still dominated the American society and white men still felt the need to control everything throughout America.

The American society after the civil war began to forge a drastic change not only throughout the south but in many parts of the north as well. Blacks ran and won political offices such as senators, congressman, and Fredrick Douglass became a U.S. Ambassador. Blacks were able to attend many all white college and obtain degrees; many became doctors, lawyers, architects, teachers, professors, etc. Blacks were able to prove that if they were given an opportunity that could succeed. With freedom Blacks began to marry for the first time under American law, as slaves were forbidden to marry, develop families and raise their own children. All Blacks for the first time was able to obtain jobs, develop careers, own homes and purchase land. Free Blacks were accepted into the United States Military Academy at West Point although many of the Black appointees went through horrific prejudice from the white cadets and white officers were still embedded with racial prejudice and bigotry. Most of the Black cadets weren't able to graduate and some who did went through internal problems that stopped their military career as officers. Most were charged with crimes, though not proven guilty was thrown out of the school and service any.

Freedom didn't last long because the North began to refrain from protecting the rights of Black citizens and the developed racial groups such as the klan that began hanging and beating up Blacks throughout the south. Then the south voted in the black codes which restricted Blacks liberties throughout the South. An the North stood by and did nothing, matter of fact discrimination became apart of the North as well in major cities like New York, New Jersey, Philadelphia, California and soon most of the North began to fall in until 1964 when President Ford signed the Civil Rights Bill given Blacks the same rights as whites under the law and making it a crime to discriminate. President Kennedy, Martin Luther King, Jr., Malcolm X. Medgar Evers, Four Black Children in a Church, a group of Black and White colleges students who were supporting voting rights for Blacks in the south were all murdered, thousands beaten, spit upon, water hosed and dogs put upon them. In many major cities their were riots from 1964 to 1967 because of police brutality, discrimination, racial tensions boiling over and mostly because the Black Youth were not like their parents who took the abuse, the youth were satisfied with being abused.

CHAPTER THIRTEEN

The Black Power Movement

What was interested was the when Whites hear Stokely Carmicheal who later changed his name to Kwame (after Kwame Nkrumah, President of Ghana) Toure (after Sanghor Toure, President of Guinea) shouted "Black Power" and Huey P. Newton and Bobby Seal shouted, "Black Power by the Power of the Gun", and Malcolm X shouted, "Black Power By Any Means Necessary". White America went into shock. I mean they were scared and the FBI, Police Departments all over the country went on high alert because white folks were truly scared that the 'niggers' were going to finally go to war. They saw that statement 'Black Power" as similar to what Patrick Henry said when he shouted out, "Give me Liberty or give me death". They thought the Blacks were going to have a revolution and they began to prepare for the biggest race war to happen in American History.

What happen was that Black Youth, college students, neighborhood kids, suburban Blacks wanted and equal piece of the pie, they weren't going to sit around and beg like their parents did for nearly five hundred years? All over the Black college and high school students were organizing, neighborhood kids were wearing black, red and green (the black power movement colors) and were developing a different consciousness, they talking about loving Black, respecting Black, no Gangs, no Drugs, no Black on Black Crime, Stop the Violence upon each other, and uniting to build a force that would force cops from beating on Blacks during arrest, stop discrimination in jobs, housing, schools, businesses, voting, military, colleges and universities, etc. They wanted the police to stop getting away with beating and murdering blacks, and they wanted due process of the law in a just way. Many organization for taking the United States to the UN and the International Court in Geneva for Human Rights violations against African-Americans.

Many Blacks went to prison and the grave yard during the Black Power Movement. Those who marched in the south for voting rights, against segregation, racist violence and law, equal citizenship were beaten, harassed and put in jail. Black youth and adults started the movement but whites joined the freedom movement throughout the south and stood with Dr. King, Jesse Jackson, and other freedom fighters. They march throughout southern cities and let racist whites know this was a time for change, and the citizens of America were not going to take it no more. Dr. King and Jesse Jackson gave electrifying speeches that went down in history. They won voting rights for Black, integration in schools, colleges, public transportation, equal opportunities in job, same pay for the same work for Blacks, and they opened the door for equality throughout America.

The Civil Rights Movement wouldn't have been successful without the Black Power movement. The racist wouldn't buckled without the realization that there were blacks with guns, black who would shot back and blacks who were willing to die and kill for freedom. Many rights saw how good Black men fought in the war and knew their abilities. Many young Black men in the Black Power Movement fought in Vietnam and were angry at the treatment of the government towards them and getting their benefits as GI's and citizens. In the 60's Black in the Inner Cities of the North were willing to die and kill for their freedom, there were street fights between militants and the police. Many police died in those fights, as well as militants. There were robberies by militants to purchase weapons. The soldiers of revolutionary groups fought and organized as freedom fighters fighting a war for freedom, justice and human rights.

The Militants (urban soldiers) weren't fighting for pay but for a just freedom. America had finally come face to face to what they feared trained soldiers fighting for their freedom. The sixties brought racism to a head and Blacks now wanted freedom, power and racial murders, arrest and beatings by racist police and white men. These actions is what motivated white and black politicians to look at the civil rights movement and say if we give blacks their liberties: voting, integration in employment, housing, schools, hospitals, etc. maybe we can offset the militant movement. Up until that point most Black politicians were just flunkies doing what the party told them to do. They had no intention of bettering the conditions of their voters who voted for them, they followed the rules of the party. Until the youth stood up in the cities an started talking about flunky Black politicians and writing about the small papers the militants published, talking about the politicians and politics of racism on the radio; whites cared nothing about Black's civil rights but when the Black youth organized in the thousands throughout America, white stood up and said Ho shit trouble!

The Black youth weren't playing, the loved Dr. King but in the north they were taking being pissed on, beaten, dog bites and most of all crackers shooting at them. The militants would shot back, and beat the racist up. In the north the black power movement took over racist colleges and closed them down until their demands were met. They organized don't integrate; don't shop at businesses who refused to drop their racist policies such only white workers and managers. They didn't sit in they refused to eat, shop and allow anybody to go in those stores, the shouted shut it down. In the north many stores folded, or decided to hire Blacks and let blacks shop without being followed or harassed for the first time. City colleges throughout the north and universities began to integrate throughout the north. In the south the whites had more control until the militants went south and started closing colleges there; fought with the racist and clearly were down with Dr. King's policy. The White's made Dr. King became the man and began to support his movement, finances came in, radio and television exposure, newspaper tag lines and major articles. When Medgar Evers was murdered the Militants wanted to go south but King urged peace and a non-violence march. Black youth were tired of racism, police violence against blacks. The police and FBI began to hunt and arrest militant leaders, arrest and kill many of them. There began a period of shot-outs between militants and police and the FBI, as they infringed on the militants liberties and force them to protect themselves. The news made the Black the criminals, when many times the cops would harass those who they knew to be members of the Black Panthers, the Republic of New Africa, Revolutionary Arm Movement, SNICK, SOBU, MOVE and other movements. Arrest them on force pretense, try to beat or shot them and the brothers and sisters would fight back, maybe even some standing around would throw bottles and fire a gun at the police. Then the police would find themselves in a melee with the neighborhood and call for back-up. Usually the militants would take the fall and get locked up, and many times in court would prove the weapon wasn't there's. Tension and violence was heavy from the 60's to the 80's, especially after Dr. King's and Malcolm X deaths. There were riots for four consecutive years 1964-68 . . . the year the government many of us political people say turned 'Heroin loose in the Black Community' and then in the 80's when 'Crack Cocaine finished the destruction of hope". Those two drugs did more damage then slavery itself. Those drugs paralyzed Blacks and a new type of slavery became history throughout our communities and it still hold control of mostly Black and Hispanic neighborhoods throughout America. We no longer labor for the white man directly but for the white power and the white pebbles in the tiny bags. Our sons and daughters, elders and grandparents are selling their souls, minds and bodies for a speedy hit. The youth who were interested in being ball players are making that money on every corner in the hood selling that powder or those pebbles (people say rock). Our beautiful young sisters and daughters are giving themselves to the cool guys on the corner with the cars and money selling drugs, only to have to raise thousands of babies single handed while those daddies are in prison. An then there's the girls who take a hit with the one she loves and turns into a dead head selling her body to take care his and hers habit. The government destroyed the most progressive movement in the Black community Black Consciousness Movement, called the Black Power Movement because doing its period drugs was down, black employment was up because wasn't about violence but families, education, employment, no drug use, eating healthy, freedom, getting rid of police brutality in the community, attending PTA meeting and caring for your children and family. Whites didn't want the Black Community to be empowered, organized, free from drugs, owning their own businesses and being involved with the quality of education for their children, so they allowed drugs to run rampant throughout the Black communities of America. You ever ask yourself why it's not in white communities like it is in the Black Community. It was put in here to destroy everything we fought for: education, jobs, health, family, housing, safety, life and our liberty. Drug addiction destroys all that. It destroys families, housing, community safety, the mind and body, the caring of the family, consciousness and conscience. Sellers think they are better then the users, but in reality they are worst they live off of somebody else suffering; selling drugs that destroy everything we've fought for the last four hundred years. Check our Arabs, Africans and Hispanics come into the black communities and buy up all the stores from the whites who used to own them. Develop their business, while black again buy and have stopped growing in the Ghetto's, complainers but not doers. Check out how the Mexicans and Whites are building all the houses, and a few of us are the mechanics. Ask yourself why? Check out our son's selling drugs on the corner, or outside of our door (I would break my son's neck if I caught him selling or using drugs) selling drugs. We know who the drug dealers are and who the users are but what are we doing about it. We're laughing at the drug users and hanging out with our son's who "give their parents cash to buy something nice". Many father's and mother's know their daughter's and son's are gang members from the clothes and tattoo's they wear and many folks allow it. Think its cool, until they get the call us from jail or he hospital, and either our child has been locked up or shot. Many people have put their house or money for bail. Many parents are participants in the drug business supplying their son's and daughter's with the cash for start up, thinking they're going to develop a constant source of money from Junior; I personally know folks who've done it. Sure you're a murder also, for all the death's those drugs cause and all the sick bodies those drugs destroy. Black folks have stopped being the niggers and bitches of white slave owners and now the bitches and niggers of drugs, drug dealers as well of the men who pay us for sex, or to maim or kill someone. We are nothing but modern day slaves. From one master to another!

When the government destroyed the Civil Rights and Black Power Movement by killing, imprisoning, buying off and using negative info to destroy them like they did to shut up Jesse Jackson they destroyed the most important elements and people in the Black Community. Blacks needed a strong powerful caring, politically astute base that wouldn't buckle under pressure. They needed educated, physically and consciously grounded folks who would stand strong against buy-out, physical threats and even imprisonment. Malcolm, Martin and Medgar was murdered, Marcus Garvey was arrested and shipped back to Jamaica, and died in England alone and broke. The Black Power fostered empowerment economically, spiritually, socially, materially, and militarily. The Orthodox Jews have a religious military who will beat you up and then hold you for the police if you come into their neighborhood and do a criminal activity. The Black Power Movement had that, the developed and fostered marriages, family and children development, business, newspapers, organization, education, no drugs, clean wholesome safe communities with neighborhood patrols. They taught self defense for men, women and youth. They organized health and educational fairs, independent schools, daycare, health clinics, opened cultural stores, bookstores, health food stores, clothing, electronic and many other independent Black businesses; fostering economic independence. The destruction of this wholesome movement is responsible of the type of dis-jointed Black communities that exist today. Drugs, gangs and a low level of expectation in many Black families lead to less organizational responsibility like attending parent teacher meeting, PTA. Parents have to play a role in their children's schools, checking out their friends, activities and making sure they're not in gangs, smoking reefer or crack, sniffing coke or heroin. We must protect our children from bad habits like not doing their homework, not studying or failing testing. Too many of our children are involved in drugs, gangs, and have guns and parents have no idea until they're called and the child is either shot or in jail. We bury too many of our children in the Black community and too many of our boys and girls in prison and going to prison. The government, states and cities are always expanding jails, and closing schools and hospitals. Why do you think that's happening? The family is one of the most important institutions for Blacks and Whites; we can not sit back and allow our youth self-destruct. Rich Black and White kids come into the ghettoes to buy their drugs, many White girls are flooding the ghettoes selling their bodies, and you can see this everyday in New York, LA, New Jersey, Baltimore, and Philadelphia, along with many other cities throughout the country. Drugs and gangs are more hip to the youth than rap music; it's destroying more of them.

We've come through nearly five centuries struggling, having racism and bigotry nearly tear this great nation apart. As citizens we've been fighting each other, dividing ourselves because of our difference rather then coming together because of our similarities. We're all human being and pretty much want the same stuff good living, nice place to live, a wonderful family and friends, a car, job, good education and enough funds to live decent. We've allowed racism and bigotry tear us apart but the beautiful thing is many of the youth today are moving away from the bigotry, racism, sexist, gay banging and religious indifference. Check out sports, music and theater, the parks, restaurants and you'll see youth of all complexions hanging out together.

CHAPTER FOURTEEN

Healing for a future

The Government, especially under Ronald Reagan was vicious in moving on the Black Power and Civil Rights Movements who wanted political and social change throughout America. The Government called out all forces to destroy the Black Power Movement and the Political and Civil Rights Organizations. Hundreds, even thousands of youth and movement organizers and followers were arrested for trumped up charges. Police would arrest and beat folks, there were shot outs, killing and the wounded, arrest of one's that survived.

Many Blacks were given long term sentences, even life in prison. Many in the movement were killed by police, FBI and the military when they were called to stop a riot, etc. When White youth aligned themselves with the Black movement they also became enemies of the state, and many of them ended up dead or in jail.

The police were used even against the Civil Rights Movement was a Non-violence movement followers could not carry and use a gun (legal under the law in most states in the sixties) for protection. The Black Power Movement advocated being armed just to deter the police from shooting an innocent person. The Black Power Movement advocated for the every citizen especially in the Black Community to carry a gun which in itself many problems. Police in those days were always stopping Blacks, especially those they thought was in the movement. The police would just stop and want to search you for no apparent reason. This in itself caused many battles between militants and the police. Black folks, were tired of police messing with them for just 'walking while black', wanting to search them. Which really did happen throughout black neighborhoods? Many people in Black communities have been victims of beatings for nothing and then arrested.

Huey P. Newton and Bobby Seal started the Panther Party to advocate against violence and false police arrest and brutality in California. The Police would always beat a black person up, especially young black men when they were arresting them. They had observed this numerous times and started to speaking about this on the college campuses and throughout black neighborhoods. The police didn't like it and started following them around, but so did black youth. This inspired them to begin organizing the youth, they used a political organization name that formerly was called the Black Panther Party but seized using the name so they took it and the party began to develop and grow into a national organization. Police in LA harassed and arrested Huey and Bobby numerous times, even persecuted Huey P. Newton for murder, which he eventually wasn't convicted for. Their fame grew and even many whites became part of the party, many rich whites who believed in self-defense and empowerment financed the movement. Their fame grew internationally and they had groups in Africa and the Caribbean. As the organization developed so did the harassment and police arrest, incarceration of Panther party members, killings of party members by police and a national government program to wipe out the Panther Party.

Black Power became not only the Political cry for the Movement but a movement in itself with people like Ron Karenga, Kwame Toure, H. Rap Brown (Imam Jamil Al-Ameen), Sister Afeni Shakur, Matulu Shakur, Imamu Amiri Baraka, Sandra Sanchez, Haki Madhbuti, Rev. Daughtry, Les Campbell (Jitu Weusi), James and Katherleen Cleaver and many more who stood up. One of the major players was the Honorable Elijah Muhammad who created the Nation of Islam with nearly a million Muslims in his Nation. They developed businesses, schools, housing, Temples, farms, factories, military the F.O.I. and newspaper the Muhammad Speaks. Another important figure was Malcolm X (El Hajj Malik El Shabazz a founder follower and National Spokesmen of the N.O.I and another was Louis Farrakhan who eventually became the National Spokesman of the N.O.I. when Malcolm was put out by Muhammad. Later the son of Elijah Muhammad began to help organize the American Muslim community and took over the N.O.I. when his father the Honorable Elijah Muhammad passed but later this group was split into two: one returning to the Notion of Islam under Farrakhan and the other the American Muslim Society under Iman Warith D. Mohammed.

From the 19th to the 21st century there has been much change in America. Black folks throughout the American society finally have reached a level of freedom and citizenship they've struggled so hard for. The very First Black President (his father is from Kenya, Africa and his mother American and Caucasian.) has been elected and throughout the political spectrum are congressmen and women, senators, assembly leaders, Mayors and we've had a leader of the Democratic Party. There have been many changes on the American horizon, but racism and bigotry still lives. Though, today there are people like President Barak Obama, former Presidents Bill Clinton and Jimmy Carter, as well, John Fitzgerald Kennedy, Lyndon Baines Johnson and James Earl Carter, Jr. who have lead this country away from nearly five centuries of outright racist polices throughout this great nation. They've dipped into the bowl of conscience unlike many of our other leaders. They didn't see people by the color of their skin but by their ideals and quality of their life. Blacks, Orientals, Amerindians, Arabs, and Hispanics have been given opportunities in every field of industry, education, science, politics, and have succeeded.

We now walk in the sunlight, with our mind and eyes wide open. We have finally redeemed Our Founding Fathers and Abraham Lincoln can finally rest in peace his job has been done. My Caucasian maternal Grandfather and African Grandmother would smile if they were living now, knowing children can finally walk through safe with a real chance. This is not a time of perfection because there are begets and racist, still those who believe whites or blacks are chosen people. Those Christians or Muslims who believe their belief is the only way and are out to destroy the unbelievers. Still, today there's ideals of love and brother/sisterhood and Buddhist, Muslims, Hindus, Christians, Gays, Straights, Yogi's, Protestants, Baptist, Sikh's and Amerindians, Polytheist, Africans, Asians, Indonesians, Americans, Caribbean's, Europeans, Orientals and others sitting together in the United Nation, the International Court, and trying to bring peace to the world. I believe our children have a chance for a better world. We've graduated and we don't put our inmates into the arena to fight to the death. There's still racism in many people's minds, still people hate other people for all kinds of reasons, and there's still racists who commit murders in America and get freed by racist jurors. The struggle continues and will always, perfection is not within us and will never be apart of humanity, that's the beauty of living; imperfection, and struggling to be better motivates us to become better and working trying to improve. Gandhi, King, Malcolm X, Kennedy, Sojourner, Harriet, Susan B., and yes George Washington and Thomas Jefferson would be proud of their America today!

In the America today keep your head up!

BIBLIOGRAPHY

Mckinley Burt, Jr., Black Inventors of AmericaCopyright ©National Book Company, a division of Educational Research Association, Portland, Oregon

Cedric Dover, American Negro Art Copyright©1960 by the National Book Company, Educational Research Association, Portland: Printed in the United States of America

Lewis V. Baldwin, There is a Balm in Gilead The Cultural Roots of Martin Luther King, Jr. Copyright©1991 Augsburg Fortress, Minneapolis, MN 55440

Harold W. Felton, MUMBET: The story of Elizabeth Freeman copyright©1970 by the University of Nebraska Foundation, Printed in the United States of America

Fight On! Mary Church Terrell's Battle for Integration: Dennis Brindell Fradin and Judith Bloom Fradin: copyright©2005, A Houghton Mifflin Company Imprint

Bigotry: copyright©1969 by Kathlyn Gay : Enslow Publishers, Inc. Printed in the United States of America

The Black Frontiersmen: copyright©1969 by J. Norman Heard and the John Day Company, Inc. New York, NY; Published in the nited States of America

Ten Blocks from the White House: Anatomy of the Washington Riots of 1968 copyright ©1968: Publisher Fredrick A. Praeger of the Washington Post: Written by Ben W. Gilbert and the staff of the Washington Post.

Eight Black American Inventors, copyright © 1972 by Robert C. Hayden and Addison-Westley: Published in the United States of America

Montezuma and the Aztecs, Nathaniel Harris copyright©1985 Wayland Publishers Ltd. New York, NY

Tuskegee Airmen by Ann Chandler Howell. Ph. D, copyright©1994 Chandler, White Publishing Co., in the United States of America

The Africa Reader: Colonial Africa—copyright© by Wilfred Cartey and Martin Kilson at Random House, Inc. published in the United States Of America and simultaneously in Canada 1970.

Encyclopedia of the United States of America at War by June A. English. Thomas D. Jones: copyright©1998 by Scholarship Inc., New York, NY

Four Took Freedom by Phillip Sterling and Raylord Logan copyright®1967 by Doubleday Company, Inc. Printed in the United States of America.

Published

Red Tail Angels: The Story of the Tuskegee Airmen of WWII by PATRICIA AND FRED MCKISSACK ©1995 in the United States of America by Walker Publishing Co., inc.

Africa's Living Arts by Anthony D. Marshall, copyright©1970 published by Franklin Watts publishing. Printed in the United States of America.

An Album of Black Americans In the Armed Forces by Major Donald L. Miller U.S. Army (R.E.T) copyright©1969 by Franklin Watts publishing. Printed in the United States of America.

Great American Negroes by Ben Richardson: copyright©1945 by Franklin Watts, Inc. Printed in the United States of the Americas.